HAMMERSMITH AND HOUNSLOW TRAMWAYS

Robert J Harley

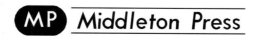

MP Middleton Press

FEATURES IN LONDON TRAMWAY CLASSICS

Rolling Stock	Title
A class. LCC	**Southwark and Deptford**
A type MET	**Waltham Cross and Edmonton**
Alexandra Palace Elec. Rly.	**Enfield and Wood Green**
B class. LCC/Bexley	**Greenwich and Dartford**
B type MET	**Stamford Hill**
Barking cars	**Ilford and Barking**
Bexley cars	**Greenwich and Dartford**
Bluebird. LCC car 1	**Camberwell and West Norwood**
C class. LCC	**Victoria and Lambeth**
Cable cars	**Clapham and Streatham**
Croydon cars	**Croydon's Tramways**
C type MET/LT	**Barnet and Finchley**
D class. LCC	**Wandsworth and Battersea**
D type MET	**Edgware and Willesden**
Dartford cars	**Greenwich and Dartford**
East Ham cars	**East Ham and West Ham**
Erith cars	**Greenwich and Dartford**
E class. LCC/LT	**Aldgate and Stepney**
E1 class. LCC/LT	**Lewisham and Catford**
E1 cars 552-601. LCC/LT	**Hampstead and Highgate**
E1 cars 1777 -1851 LCC/LT	**Clapham and Streatham**
E3 class. LCC/LT	**Camberwell and West Norwood**
E3 class. Leyton/LT	**Walthamstow and Leyton**
E type MET/LT	**Enfield and Wood Green**
Experimental Tramcars MET/LUT/LT	**Barnet and Finchley**
F class. LCC	**Embankment and Waterloo**
F type MET	**Waltham Cross and Edmonton**
G class. LCC	**Embankment and Waterloo**
G type MET/LT	**Stamford Hill**
Gravesend & Northfleet cars	**North Kent**
H class (works). LCC/LT	**Eltham and Woolwich**
H type MET/LT	**Stamford Hill**
Horse cars. North Met./LCC	**Aldgate and Stepney**

HR2 class. LCC/LT	**Camberwell and W Norwood**
Ilford cars	**Ilford and Barking**
K class (works) LCC/LT	**Waltham Cross and Edmonton**
L class (works). LCC/LT	**Holborn and Finsbury**
L/1 class (works) LCC/LT	**Clapham and Streatham**
Leyton cars	**Walthamstow and Leyton**
LT car 2	**Wandsworth and Battersea**
LUT car 341	**Kingston and Wimbledon**
M class LCC/LT	**Greenwich and Dartford**
Petrol electric cars. LCC	**Southwark and Deptford**
SMET cars	**Croydon's Tramways**
S2 type LUT	**Shepherds Bush and Uxbridge**
T type LUT	**Kingston and Wimbledon**
Trailer cars LCC	**Clapham and Streatham**
UCC type MET/LT	**Edgware and Willesden**
U type LUT	**Hammersmith and Hounslow**
Walthamstow cars	**Walthamstow and Leyton**
West Ham cars	**East Ham and West Ham**
Works cars MET	**Waltham Cross and Edmonton**
Works cars LUT	**Hammersmith and Hounslow**
X type LUT	**Shepherds Bush and Uxbridge**

Miscellaneous	
Advertising on tramcars	**Aldgate and Stepney**
Conduit system	**Embankment and Waterloo**
Overhead wiring	**Edgware and Willesden**
Power supply	**Walthamstow and Leyton**
Request stops	**Victoria and Lambeth**
Section boxes	**Eltham and Woolwich**
Track layouts - single & loops	**Stamford Hill**
Track Construction and Maintenance	**Barnet and Finchley**
Tram tours	**Holborn and Finsbury**
Upstairs - Downstairs	**Hammersmith and Hounslow**

First Published July 1999

ISBN 1 901706 33 8

© Middleton Press, 1999

Design Deborah Esher
David Pede

Published by
Middleton Press
Easebourne Lane
Midhurst, West Sussex
GU29 9AZ
Tel: 01730 813169
Fax: 01730 812601

Printed & bound by Biddles Ltd,
Guildford and Kings Lynn

CONTENTS

Hammersmith	1
Shepherds Bush	15
Chiswick	18
Kew Bridge	34
Kew to Richmond Horse Tramway	46
Brentford	49
Brentford, Half Acre to Hanwell	63
Isleworth and Hounslow	71
LUT Works Cars Miscellany	94
Upstairs - Downstairs	101
LUT Type U	116
Progress - Too Little, Too Late!	120

INTRODUCTION AND ACKNOWLEDGEMENTS

This second volume detailing the erstwhile LUT system owes much to the contributions of the following experts: John Gillham who supplied factual information, Dave Jones, Curly Cross, Pat Chappelle and John Meredith who have lent pictures from their respective photo archives, Terry Russell who has made available another of his excellent car plans and John Gent who has loaned many rare views dating from the turn of the twentieth century.

Those readers desiring more information on the London United Tramways should consult the splendid two volume series by C.S.Smeeton, and the book "London United Tramways - A History 1894-1933" by Geoffrey Wilson.

My thanks go to Rosy Thacker of the John Price Memorial Library at the National Tramway Museum for her assistance in supplying articles from various trade journals. Tickets are from Godfrey Croughton's collection.

LondonTransport timetables and maps are reproduced by kind permission of LT Museum, Covent Garden.

GEOGRAPHICAL SETTING

The routes described in this book served the suburbs of West London north of the River Thames. In tram days the local authority was the County of Middlesex; the county town was Brentford. Since 1965 larger London Boroughs have taken over the functions of the former County of Middlesex.

HISTORICAL BACKGROUND

Horse trams of the West Metropolitan Company were opened for business along the Goldhawk Road on 18th March 1882. The service connected Shepherds Bush Green with Young's Corner, Chiswick. A further extension, opened on 16th December 1882, saw trams reach the new terminus on the north side of Kew Bridge. Unfortunately a connecting link to the south side terminus was never constructed, and the route to Richmond, opened on 17th April 1883, remained in permanent isolation from the rest of the system. A further line followed from Young's Corner to Hammersmith, and in 1894 the old West Metropolitan was absorbed into the London United Tramways. This was a concern which had bold plans for the future of London's street transport. These schemes were put into effect from 4th April 1901 when electric traction superseded equine power on the Shepherds Bush and Hammersmith routes to Kew Bridge. Thereafter progress was speedy, and passenger services to The Bell at Hounslow were inaugurated on 6th July 1901. A short extension from The Bell to The Hussar at Hounslow followed on 13th August 1902.

Originally the LUT was conceived as a vast enterprise with projected lines past Hounslow to Staines, Cranford, Hanworth and Sunbury. Thus the end of the rails at Hounslow Heath was considered as a temporary halt to a tramway network serving the Staines Road. Reality soon set

in and inspite of new lines from Busch Corner to Twickenham, opened on the same day as The Hussar extension, and from Studland Street to Askew Arms, opened on 1st June 1904, grandiose plans to add to the LUT's mileage were quietly shelved. No LUT car ever did reach Staines.

The LUT was acquired by the London and Suburban Traction Co Ltd on 1st January 1913. This brought a respite from financial problems, but the LUT had to face large scale track renewals and a rapidly ageing fleet. Lines in the Borough of Hammersmith were later transferred to

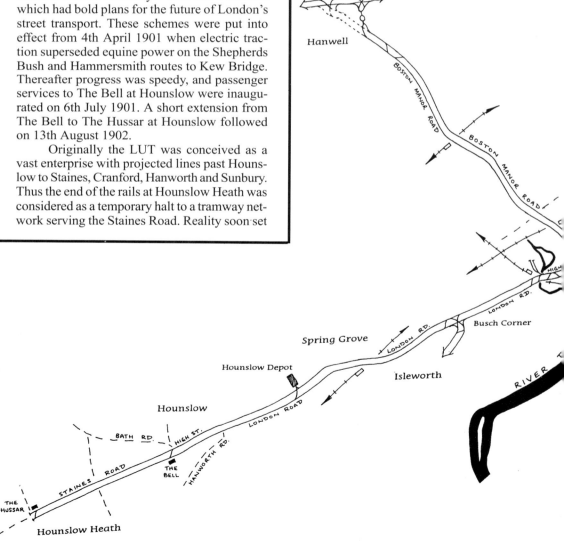

the London County Council, who also took possession of Chiswick Depot. On 24th April 1922 LCC cars commenced trial runs over former LUT tracks. LCC service 26 was extended to Kew Bridge on 2nd May 1922. LUT cars on route 89 were extended to Putney on 28th November 1928.

All was not well with the tramways and the LUT management formulated plans for the partial replacement of railed vehicles by trolleybuses. This policy was agressively pursued by the next owners, London Transport who arrived on the scene on 1st July 1933. The trunk routes from Shepherds Bush to Hounslow and from Hammersmith to Hampton Court were converted on 27th October 1935. The lines from Hammersmith to Acton followed on 5th April 1936. The last car on the former LCC tramway which crossed Hammersmith Broadway, departed on 11th September 1937, after which the trolleybus reigned supreme.

Electric street traction came to an end in 1961/62 when local trolleybus services were ousted by diesel buses.

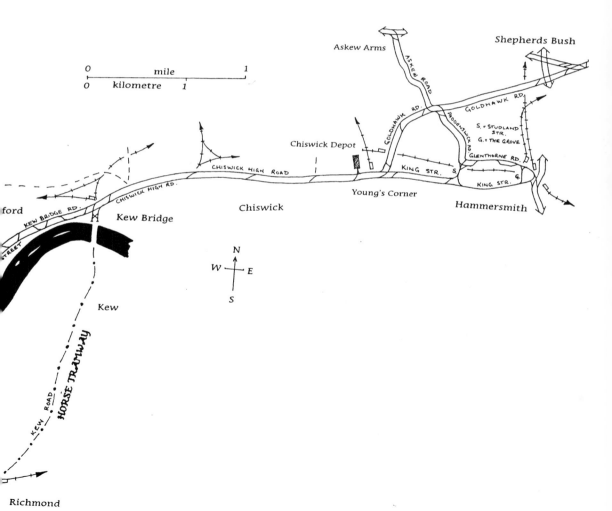

HAMMERSMITH

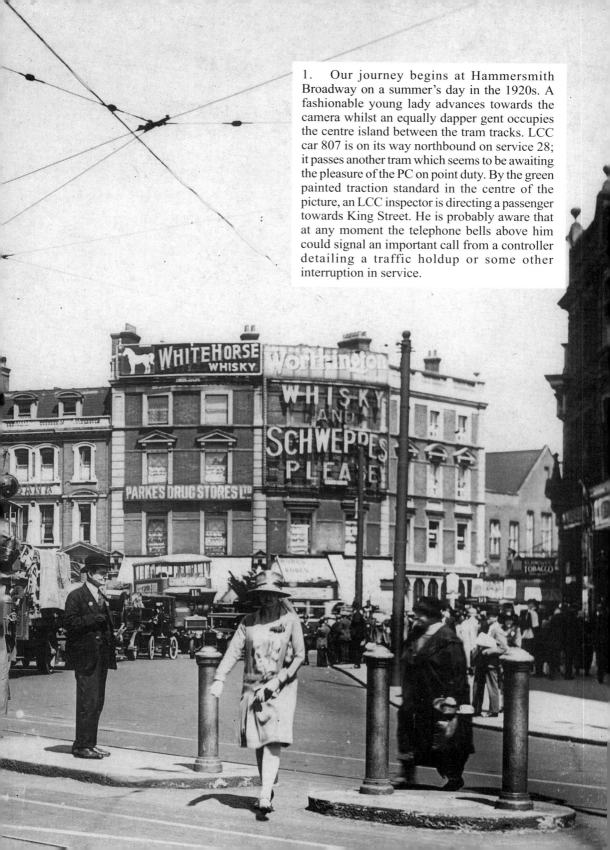

1. Our journey begins at Hammersmith Broadway on a summer's day in the 1920s. A fashionable young lady advances towards the camera whilst an equally dapper gent occupies the centre island between the tram tracks. LCC car 807 is on its way northbound on service 28; it passes another tram which seems to be awaiting the pleasure of the PC on point duty. By the green painted traction standard in the centre of the picture, an LCC inspector is directing a passenger towards King Street. He is probably aware that at any moment the telephone bells above him could signal an important call from a controller detailing a traffic holdup or some other interruption in service.

55 Through Fare **2d.**	**BRENTFORD**, Boston Manor Station, Boston Road, **HANWELL**, Time 13 mins. *Service : Weekdays 7½ mins., Sundays 10 mins. Extended via West Ealing to* **EALING**, *during Weekday Rush Hours.* Time 22 mins. *Service : 7½ mins.* Fare **4d.**
57 Through Fare **6d.**	**HOUNSLOW**, Isleworth Station, Busch Corner, Brentford, Kew Bridge, Gunnersbury, Chiswick, Turnham Green, Youngs Corner, **SHEPHERDS BUSH** Time 40 mins. *Service : 8 mins. Works jointly with Services 63 and 67 between Kew Bridge and Youngs Corner.*
63 Through Fare **3d.**	**KEW BRIDGE**, Gunnersbury, Chiswick, Turnham Green, Youngs Corner, **SHEPHERDS BUSH,** Time 19 mins. *Service : Weekdays 5 mins., Sundays 10 mins. Note.—This service is extended during week-day rush hours to Isleworth Fire Station (via Brentford and Busch Corner),* Time 33 mins. *Service : 8 mins. Fare 5d. Works jointly with Services 57 and 67 and L.C.C. Service 26 between Kew Bdg. & Youngs Corner.*
67 Through Fare **10d.** *Cheap Return **1/-**	**HAMPTON COURT**, Hampton, Bushey Park, Fulwell, Twickenham, Isleworth, Busch Corner, Brentford, Kew Bridge, Gunnersbury, Chiswick, Turnham Green, Youngs Corner, **HAMMERSMITH,** Time 61 mins. *Service : Weekdays 6 mins., Sundays 8 mins. *Cheap Return Fares are also issued intermediately on this route on Weekdays (Public Holidays Excepted) after 10 a.m., and Sundays all day. Works jointly with Services 57 and 63 and L.C.C. Service 26 between Kew Bridge and Youngs Corner.*
89 Through Fare **5d.** Return Fare **9d.**	**ACTON**, ActonVale, **HAMMERSMITH**, thence Weekdays only to Fulham Palace Road, **PUTNEY,** Time 34 mins. *Service : Acton and Hammersmith, Weekdays 3 mins.,Sundays 4½mins.; Hammersmith and Putney, Weekdays only, 8 mins.*

2.   We now experience an altogether more sombre mood than was apparent in the previous view. Here a "volunteer" driver is proceeding gingerly across the Broadway. The crowds of onlookers may have some sympathy for those who have withdrawn their labour, for this scene depicts one aspect of the 1926 General Strike. Service 30 and other LCC operations south of this location are covered in companion volume *Wandsworth and Battersea Tramways.*

List of LUT services as at 1929.

3.   We traverse the Broadway into LUT territory where we espy car 141 at the corner of Beadon Road. Note Hammersmith Station on the joint Metropolitan/GWR section to Paddington and the City. The station dates from 1864 and electric trains were inaugurated on 5th November 1906, over five years after the LUT electric trams had appeared in the street outside.

4.   A Hansom cab waits in the station forecourt as car 270 is about to negotiate the eastern end of the Hammersmith terminal loop. The tram's indicator has already been turned to read HAMPTON COURT.

5. Car 279 is in Beadon Road. Between the photographer and the tram is the triangular junction with The Grove. Tracks along this latter thoroughfare were employed at peak times to relieve congestion at the terminus. Car 279 was originally type W, but was top covered in 1910-11 and was reclassified type U.

6. Proof of the immense popularity of the trams is displayed in this view of car 235 loading in Beadon Road. Due to the fine weather seats on the top deck seem to be at a premium! At least one potential customer has a spot of fishing in mind as he waits to board.

7. Our next visitor to Beadon Road is this smartly turned out, but rather antiquated looking tramcar which is working service 89 to Acton. Note the through booking facilities advertised below the top deck windows. This "integrated fare structure" was way ahead of its time, and encouraged many LUT passengers to forsake competing suburban railways in their journeys from the western suburbs to offices in the West End and City.

8. Car 267 waits at the same place as the previous view. The date is probably around the late 1920s. Note the trolley rope tied to the stanchion on the "Robinson" type staircase. This form of ascent to the upper saloon was particularly favoured by the LUT, in contrast to the conventional half turn variety as used by most other tramway operators. Its nickname refers to Sir James Clifton Robinson who was the dynamic managing director of the LUT.

9. Round the corner in King Street a couple of policeman seem to be curious about an influx of trippers who have planned a day out at Hampton Court. Whatever the outcome of this little incident, car 155 will be able to stop quickly as the warning triangle on the dash informs us of EIGHT WHEEL BRAKES. That should put paid to the flight of any fugitives from the law.

10. The conductor of car 303 supervises a full load as his charge edges its way through Hammersmith. The crowd swallowing capacities of tramcars were well known and most sympathetic conductors would always find room for "one more on top" if the need arose.

11. The motorman of car 16 looks rather grim as he slows his tram to walking pace. This was necessary to prevent dewirements when, in this case, the trolley wheel was passing over points (a "frog" in technical parlance) in the overhead. This is winter and for the time being only one hardy soul has braved the elements to sit on the top deck.

12. This animated scene was probably taken in the summer of 1935, a few months before trolleybuses first appeared on King Street. The driver of the Nugget Boot Polish van knows his highway code and has halted to let passengers cross from the pavement to the waiting car 2326, now in full London Transport red and cream livery. The exit from The Grove is by Burton Tailoring.

13. Glenthorne Road is north of and roughly parallel to King Street. Car 148 was a member of type X and survived into LT days as a works car attached to Hanwell Depot. Note the neat and stylish overhead suspension work and the ornate tracery on the traction standards. The LUT was nothing if not lavish in its equipping of its pioneer routes.

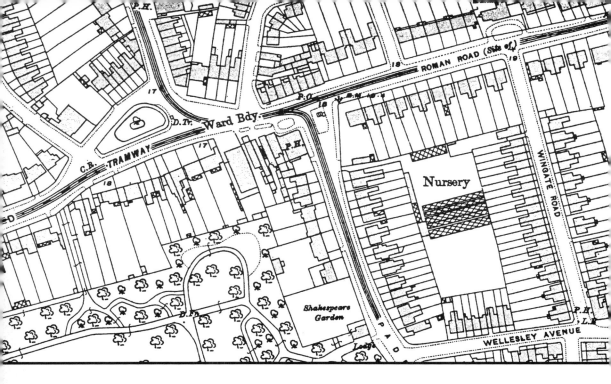

14. Lines in Paddenswick Road joined Hammersmith with Goldhawk Road. The motorman of car 209 shuts off power as he passes under a section feed. This avoided possible damage caused by arcing. Car 209 first appeared in white livery, but this was altered to yellow and cream, as seen here. About 1909 it was repainted red to conform with the colours of the bulk of the fleet. Aside from the "chariot of the people" local transport for the wealthy still consisted of a carriage and top hatted coachman.

15. Askew Road connects Goldhawk Road with Uxbridge Road. Cars 75 and 91 were originally type Z, but were allocated to type Y after they were given top covers in 1910-11. We observe yet another section feed above car 75, these occurred every half mile and they supplied 550 volts direct current to the overhead.

16. It is recorded that after commencement of electric services in 1901, takings at the Shepherds Bush Empire rose accordingly. The new form of transport was instrumental in widening the horizons of working people. For a few pennies a family could now travel out of the urban grime to enjoy the sunshine and countryside. It is worth remembering that in 1907, when this postcard was mailed the only choice for the poorest of the capital's citizens was one between Shanks's Pony (walking) and taking the tram. Train and bus fares were just too expensive.

17. On the south side of Shepherds Bush Green, looking east, we see car 321 resplendent in its Venetian red and white livery. Roadworks in those days were protected by wooden stands and hurdles - somewhat of a contrast to the hideous plastic cones which now clutter up our streets.

CHISWICK

18.   King Street joins Goldhawk Road at Young's Corner. This view was taken shortly after the introduction of electric traction. On the left of the picture is a metal pole supporting a lamp which indicated to motormen the direction of the points on the London bound line. A green light confirmed the points were set for Goldhawk Road and Shepherds Bush, a white light assured passage straight ahead to King Street and Hammersmith.

19. Time has moved on and we now witness Young's Corner about the era of the First World War. Car 74 is on a routine trip to Hounslow and has just crossed the county boundary from London into Middlesex.

20. May 1935 marked the celebrations of the Silver Jubilee of King George V and Queen Mary, hence the patriotic decorations festooning the building behind car 2345. This was the last summer of tramway operation at Young's Corner.

21. Many readers will remember the trolleybuses, and this view is a nostalgic look back to the days before May 1962 when London went "all diesel". Route 657 replaced tram route 57 in October 1935.

22. Chiswick High Road was served by trams for over thirty years. Cars 6 and 83 are seen here in their Edwardian heyday. They are passing the LUT offices and the entrance to Chiswick Depot.

23. Car 6 still sports its original wire mesh lifeguard as it stands on the entrance track to Chiswick Power Station and Car Shed. The LUT head office is to the right of the picture.

24. The first occupants of Chiswick Depot were horse trams such as car 50 which was one of a batch of ten built by the LUT at Chiswick in 1896. It is quite probable that it used the underframe of an older Stephenson built car dating back to the 1870s.

25. The Central Power Station and Car Sheds were the subject of extensive coverage in the technical press. Much attention was paid to architectural details and the ornamental design of many interior fittings won much praise from contemporary critics. The buildings passed to LCC ownership in 1917 and from 1922 the depot was used for 30 LCC cars which worked mostly on service 26. The site was vacated by trams in May 1932 and the building subsequently had a chequered history. One of its latest incarnations is as Stamford Brook Bus Garage.

Extract from 1915 survey of Chiswick Depot. Please see *Willesden Junction to Richmond* for details of the railway stations.

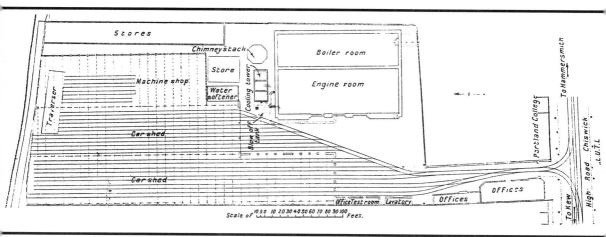

STAMFORD BROOK
COMMON
1
2·145

26. A steam lorry, registered M 1768, leads a procession of horse drawn vehicles along Chiswick High Road. Car 87 lets off several passengers before going on its way. Note the running number 2 attached to the staircase.

27. This postcard view was also issued in a realistic coloured version which featured car 263 in royal blue livery, whereas sister car 35 was depicted in red. A bright and cheerful prospect was therefore guaranteed for the onlookers on the High Road. In fact there were trams galore along this stretch - will such pollution free days ever return?

————————→

28. Carters often positioned their wheels over the tramlines so as to experience a smoother ride. The wagon shown here has just about enough space to squeeze past car 34, but one suspects it won't be long before a sharp burst of the gong from a following tramcar causes the whole contraption to veer towards the kerb.

————————→

29. Experimental tramcar 350, nicknamed Poppy, appeared on LUT tracks from 1928. This vehicle was a regular performer on service 57 which traversed Chiswick. The tram itself was a brave attempt at modernisation, and as can be seen, the designers tried to marry traditional features with the avant garde such as platform doors and separate driver's cabins. Because of antiquated police regulations the bulk of London's trams and buses were not equipped with windscreens until the 1930s.

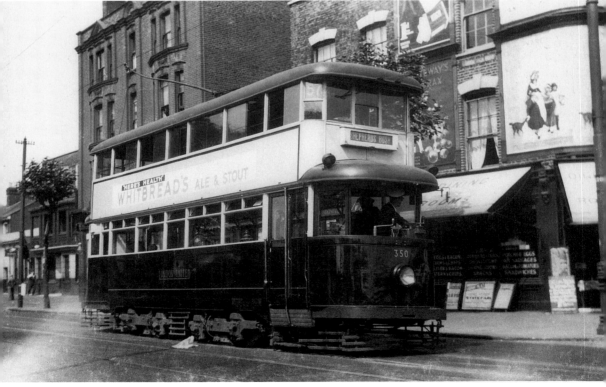

30. We are now looking west in the vicinity of Chiswick Park Station, with the Old Pack Horse Inn on the right. Car 35 is seen in "as delivered" condition as it passes the end of Acton Lane. Chiswick Park Station on the District Railway was opened in 1879 as Acton Green.

———————▶

31. Car 2345 is encountered again, this time at the junction of Chiswick High Road, Great West Road and Gunnersbury Avenue. It is working route 63 from Kew Bridge to Shepherds Bush. The tram in front, a former member of the LCC fleet, is straying somewhat farther afield as it heads for the Borough/London Bridge on service 26. On the extreme left of the picture a Green Line coach on the Windsor service accelerates out of shot. In the background is the premises of the Elkington Carriage Company. Nowadays this intersection is the site of a large roundabout and associated slip roads leading to the M4 flyover.

———————▶

32. Just west of the road junction we encounter car 205, on the Hampton Court to Hammersmith service 67. This tram was delivered in 1902, and inspite of receiving a top cover, it still looks its age. All in all it is not much of a match for the competing motor buses with their pneumatic tyres and cushioned seats. LUT car 205 was renumbered 2362 by London Transport and it was scrapped in July 1936.

33. Car 83 is pictured on Chiswick High Road near the entrance to Wellesley Road in the first weeks of the system. Maybe this was one of the official parties on opening day.

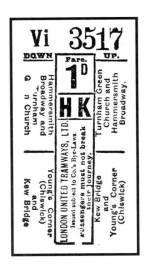

KEW BRIDGE

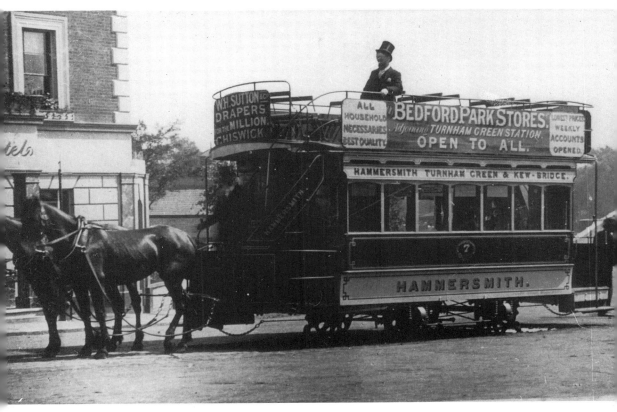

34. West Metropolitan car 7 pauses at the terminus by Kew Bridge before the return trip to Hammersmith.

35. The swansong of horse traction is reflected here at the end of the line. New traction standards have already been planted in preparation for the coming electric shock which will dispose of our four legged friends and all the paraphernalia which went with them - stables, hay stores, vets' bills and manure heaps.

36. A crowd of interested spectators observe the comings and goings of the new electric trams. At Kew Bridge there was a scissors crossover which expedited terminal movements. The building on the left behind car 94 forms part of the LSWR Kew Bridge Station which was opened for traffic on 22nd August 1849. The trams would prove formidable competition to the suburban railway trains.

37. Nobody seems to want to disturb the peace of car 2411 as it basks in the summer sunshine. The crew will presumably turn up soon to continue the journey to Hampton Court. A notice in one lower saloon window informs us NEAR BRENTFORD FOOTBALL GROUND; no doubt the trams transported many fans in this 1934-35 season when the local team won the Football League Second Division and achieved a place amongst the elite of the country.

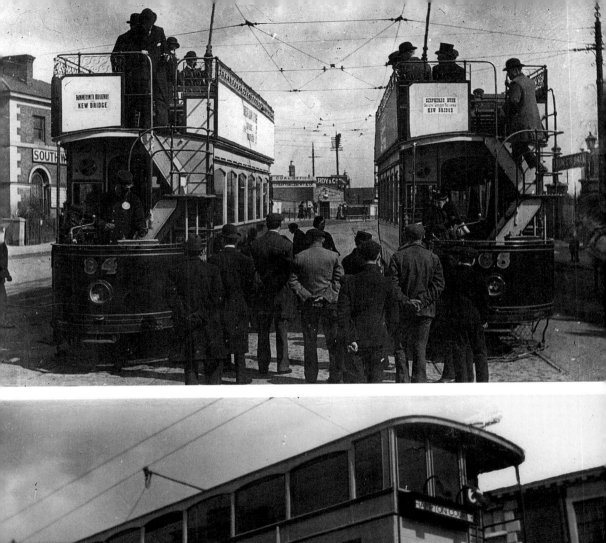

→

38. A contrast of body styles is seen at Kew Bridge terminus as former LCC car 583, experimentally painted in blue by London Transport, shares the right of way with LUT car 155.

39. The Star & Garter Hotel forms the backdrop to another brace of trams in this September 1925 view. This time the LCC car on service 26 appears in the more traditional brown and cream livery. The LUT car is arrayed in red and cream with the company crest on the waist panel. The LIPTON'S advert is a dark green background with white lettering.

→

40. "Poppy" rests at the terminus which has now gained a rather utilitarian inspectors' cabin at the end of the rails. The North London Railway offered an alternative route to the City from Kew Bridge - see the *Willesden Junction to Richmond* album.

41. Car 320 belonged to LUT type T and had started its career in the Kingston area. A study of this type, plus a picture of car 320 in original condition can be consulted in the companion volume *Kingston and Wimbledon Tramways*.

42. Prominent in this picture postcard are the ornamental stone drinking fountain, the Edwardian street lamps and the solid traction pole anchoring the overhead wires. On the back of the card, in a missive postmarked - Brentford 13th September 1915 - the writer bewailed the fact that she had to walk home from Ealing because there were no buses running - perhaps she should have taken the tram!

43. For those of a technical disposition, car 210 seen here, was built by Milnes in 1902 and was classified type W. It had Brill 22E trucks, Westinghouse equipment and two 25 hp motors. In 1910-11 it received a top cover and was reclassified type U. It was reconditioned in 1926-7 with higher power motors and magnetic brakes. On passing into LT ownership it was renumbered 2363 and it was scrapped in August 1936.

44. In the early 1930s trams and other "more flexible" motor traffic were seen as increasingly incompatible, hence the search by the powers that be for a viable alternative to the railbound tramcar. Unfortunately noboby could predict a future where all the road space would be taken up by lorries, vans and private motorists. Here we are looking west from Kew Bridge at car 255 which is tackling the grade up to the railway bridge.

45. The architectural wonders of Kew Bridge Pumping Station are in full view. These buildings now house a splendid museum devoted to the great days of the Metropolitan Water Board. Steam driven beam engines function on site and the whole place is a tribute to the confidence of Victorian engineering.

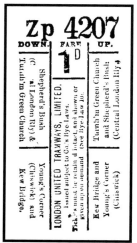

Zp 4207

DOWN.   FARE   UP.

1D

LONDON UNITED TRAMWAYS, LIMITED.

Issued subject to Co's Bye-Laws.

Ticket must be retained intact, and shown or given up on demand (see Bye-Law 40).

DOWN.
Shepherd's Bush
(C'al London Rly &
Turnh'm Green Church

UP.
Turnh'm Green Church
and Shepherd's Bush
(Central London Rly.)

Young's Corner
(Chiswick) and
Kew Bridge.

Kew Bridge and
Young's Corner
(Chiswick)

46. The Kew to Richmond section of the LUT was one of London's tramway backwaters. Horse cars ran every 12 minutes and the fare from Kew Green, seen here, to Richmond, Church Road was one penny.

47. Car 22 was the last horse tram on this branch, and history records that it entered the depot in Richmond at 11.20pm on 20th April 1912. The line was never electrified.

48. This view outside Richmond Depot was reputedly taken on the last day of the horse trams. Certainly everyone seems intent on giving the old warriors a good send off. This was all very different from the day in April 1883 when the first tram had departed on its maiden run.

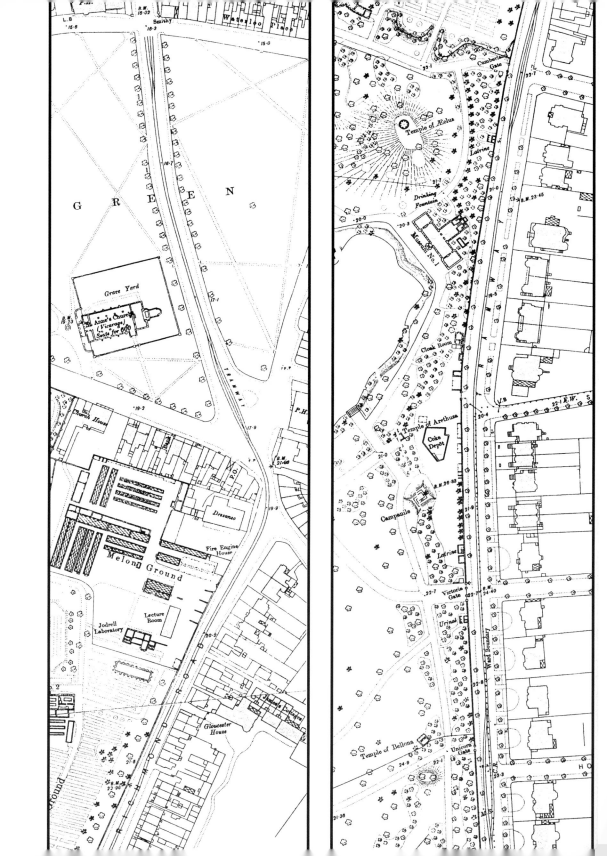

Left panel labels:

L.B · 15·6
Smithy · 16·3
B.M. 16·02
Waterloo Place
15·0

G R E E N

16·7

Grave Yard

B.M. 23·0

St. Anne's Church
(Vicarage)
Seats for 900

17·1

TRAMWAY

Church House

Bank

P.O.

19·2

P.H.

17·9

B.M. 21·66

Dressense

19·9

Fire Engine
House

Melon Ground

Lecture
Room

Jodrell
Laboratory

20·2

27·8

Gloucester
House

B.M. 22·96

Right panel labels:

Cumberland
Gate

22·7

Temple of Æolus

Latrine

Drinking
Fountain

21·1

21·0

B.M. 23·45

20·0

20·3

Museum No. 1

19·5

W A L K

Cloak Room

20·4

22·7 B.W. S

V.B.

Temple of Arethusa

Coke
Depôt

21·0

B.M. 26·83

Campanile

Latrine

21·9

Victoria Gate · B.M. 24·40

22·7

Urinal

Ward Boundary

22·93

Temple of Bellona

24·9

22·1

Unicorn
Gate

23·3

21·36

H O

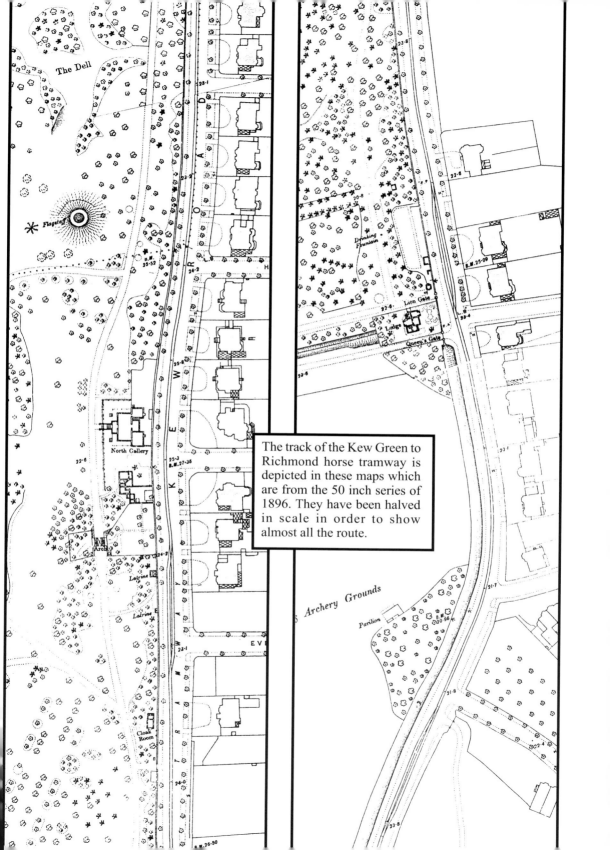

The track of the Kew Green to Richmond horse tramway is depicted in these maps which are from the 50 inch series of 1896. They have been halved in scale in order to show almost all the route.

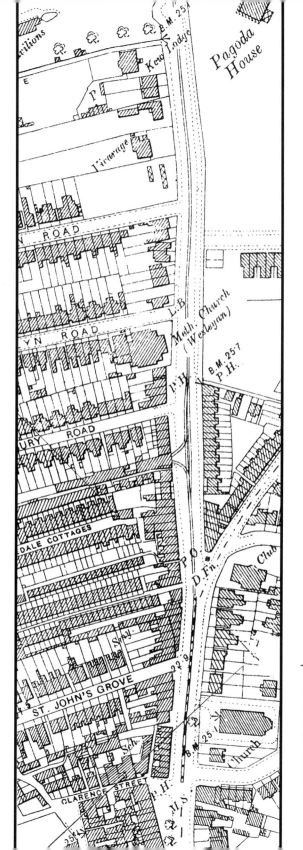

49. Brentford High Street attained a certain notoriety in London tramway circles because of the restricted width of the thoroughfare which necessitated numerous facing and trailing crossovers. Thus, trams could manoeuvre past parked carts and wagons. Car 92, ahead of car 249, already seems to be in the throes of running "wrong road" past an obstruction.

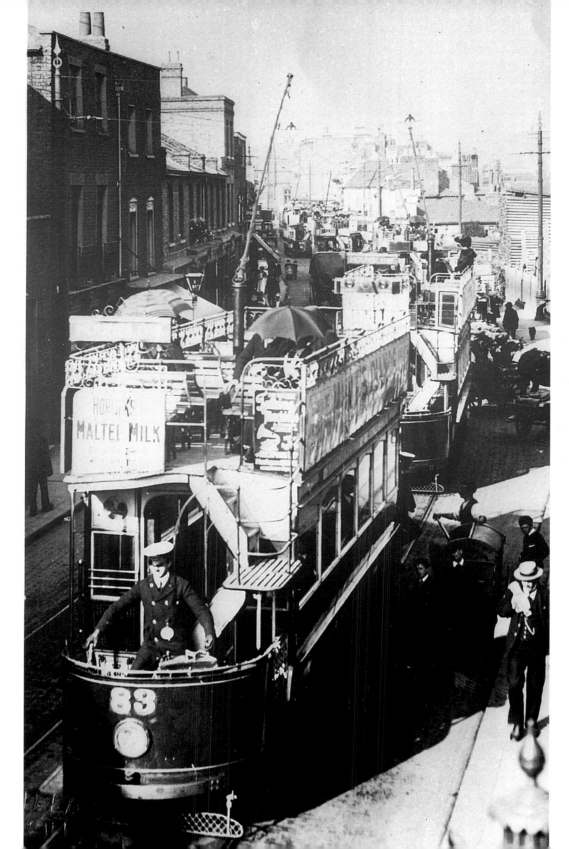

50. As befits a main tramway artery, two lines of tramcars manage to fill most of the available road space. The sun was obviously too strong for several ladies on the top deck of car 83.

51. The local picture postcard publisher definitely saw commercial potential in the local traffic jams. A series of cards was printed, each view captioned with a humorous aside. This one reads ONCE SEEN NEVER FORGOTTEN....At least in those days the good folk of Brentford had their High Street full of non polluting public transport!

52. Another view from the same stable as the previous card. This one features the sentiments OH FATHER WHAT A BIG TRAMWAY DEPOT! ITS NOT A TRAMWAY DEPOT MY CHILD - ITS ONLY BRENTFORD HIGH STREET.

53. This picture was taken just after view no.50. One can see that the wagon adjacent to car 83 is effectively blocking one line of traffic.

→

54. At the western end of Brentford High Street we observe car 6 which on this day has a fairly clear passage past the shops and hostelries. Thirty years separate this view and the following picture.

→

55. This is the location depicted previously, but the tram only has a few months of active service ahead of it. In a short time the peace of the High Street will be disturbed by crews erecting the new overhead wires for trolleybus routes 657 and 667.

56. Brentford High Street in the 1920s offers us a fine study of various period architecture with different window and shop front styles. Almost lost amongst the red brick is a freshly painted LUT traction standard. These were manufactured from three lengths of steel tubing. They reached a height of 25ft. 6ins/7772mm, and the spear head finial which surmounted the pole was 18 inches/457mm in length. The solid octagonal casting which protected the pole base was 4ft. 6ins/1371mm high and 16ins/406mm across.

57. We look east along Brentford High Street near its junction with Half Acre. Car 2342 is passing The Castle as it endeavours to catch up with car 2362. At least towards the end of the tramway era some parts of the carriageway had been widened from their former constricted state.

58. Outside the Red Lion a hay wagon manages to hold up car 184 which is full of day trippers.

59. Car 2523 (ex-LUT car 173) looks more and more like a museum piece as it retains its open top and uncanopied platforms. Such a sight was hardly an encouragement to would-be passengers, and the replacing trolleybuses offered a standard of comfort which many trams could not match.

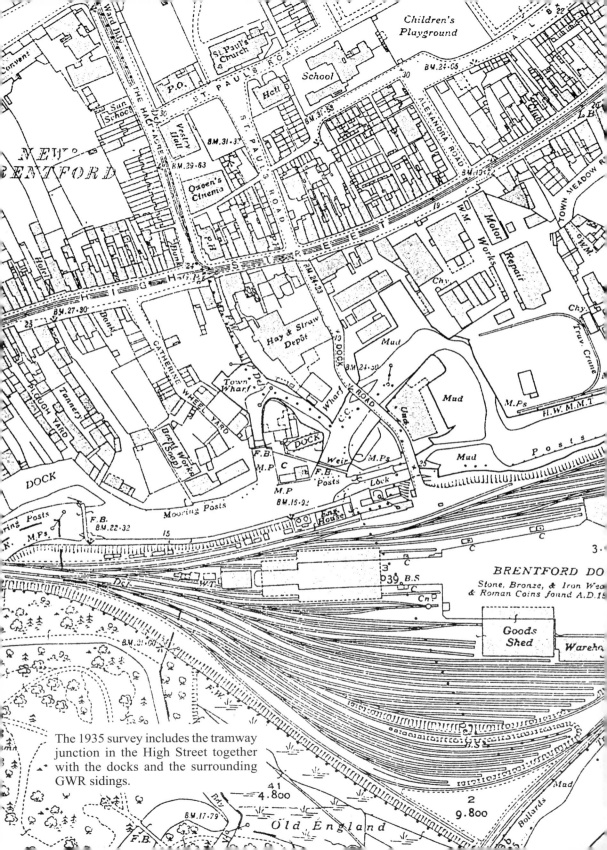

The 1935 survey includes the tramway junction in the High Street together with the docks and the surrounding GWR sidings.

60. At the western end of the High Street the tracks hugged the pavement as they traversed the canal bridge over the River Brent and Grand Junction Canal. A set of rails leads off left to the entrance of Brentford Permanent Way Yard.

61. This is the entrance to Brentford PW Yard; the impression is enhanced by the elegant short bracket arm and the solid, functional gatehouse and office in the centre of this May 1929 picture. One presumes the notice on the barrier was not heeded by tram drivers who only had a gong at their disposal.

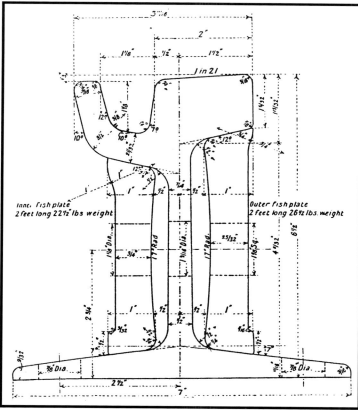

62. The stack of rails on the left was probably paid for by the LCC who had to loan money to the LUT to keep it in the tramway business. Notice also the piles of granite setts and Jarrah woodblocks which were employed as street paving along the tram tracks. The GWR branch is on the left.

Rail section as used by the LUT.

63. The trolley of car 117 is swung in preparation for the return trip along Boston Manor Road to Hanwell. There is so little road traffic about that the photographer can position his tripod in the middle of the junction with no fear for his safety. From the mud gouged out of the tracks in the foreground, it would seem that they are little used.

64. Route numbers were introduced by the LUT in 1912/13. Hanwell to Brentford became route 55. Towards the end of the LUT era, a motorman poses at Half Acre before setting off with car 27 on the thirteen minute journey to Hanwell. The through fare was tuppence!

65. Car 117 was obviously the Hanwell shuttle tram on the day the photographer chose to record the scene for posterity. We are looking north from Half Acre towards Boston Manor Road.

66. Even on lightly trafficed routes no expense was spared by the LUT, and whereas other provincial tramway operators may have used single track and loops, the London United Electric Tramways Company lived up to its billing. The company directors paid out a large part of shareholders' funds on expensive road widening schemes before rails could be laid. The double tracks in Boston Manor Road which are occupied by car 117 bear witness to the lavish plans of the LUT.

67. "Rus in Urbe" could be the title of this scene, as car 37 passes through a countrified part of Boston Road. So much of this view harks back to a lost age, when the pace of life here on the outskirts of the metropolis was slower and more measured. Even the fine elm trees, like the one in the background, have now vanished from many areas of the home counties, most of the species having been decimated by disease in the late 1960s.

────────────►

68. The fossilized tracks in the foreground once connected Lower Boston Road to Uxbridge Road. They were last used around 1910 and were removed in 1930. Meanwhile car 32 of type Y swings along Boston Road to traverse the single track leading to the terminus at Hanwell.

────────────►

69. The fellow in the flat hat rounds car 13 in order to put his child's pushchair on the front platform by the motorman. In the background is the main Uxbridge Road route which is fully described in *Shepherds Bush and Uxbridge Tramways*.

70. Before we leave Hanwell, we take one more look at shuttle car 27. Route 55 was one of the shortest in London, ironically after it was replaced by trolleybus 655 on Sunday, 13th December 1936, the new 655 service ran from Acton to Hammersmith. Over the years it was progressively extended so that at 14.8 miles/23.8kms it became London's longest trolleybus service.

ISLEWORTH AND HOUNSLOW

71. We look east along London Road to observe car 273 passing the ornamental Lion Gates at Syon Park. This was formerly the residence of the Dukes of Northumberland; Syon House was granted in 1603 to Henry Percy, 9th Duke of Northumberland.

72. In modern parlance car 2389 would be well past its "sell by date", but it soldiers on and the motorman has just applied power to switch the points at Busch Corner. The "skate" on the overhead sends an electrical impulse to the point motors. Trams on route 57 coasted at this point, whilst those on service 67 copied car 2389.

73. Busch Corner itself, and car 2365 pulls away in the direction of Brentford, whilst the other road users wait for the green light.

74. The fountain at Spring Grove was donated by the Pears Soap Company. Spring Grove Road goes off to the left in this pre First World War scene.

———→

75. Looking in the opposite direction to the previous view, we catch sight of car 40 as it rounds the corner in London Road.

76. Hounslow Depot opened in 1901 and contained ten tracks. As can be seen from the entrance gates, the LUT's solid style suggested that everything was built to last. Unfortunately, the last trams left in October 1935.

Extract from the 1915 survey showing Hounslow Depot.

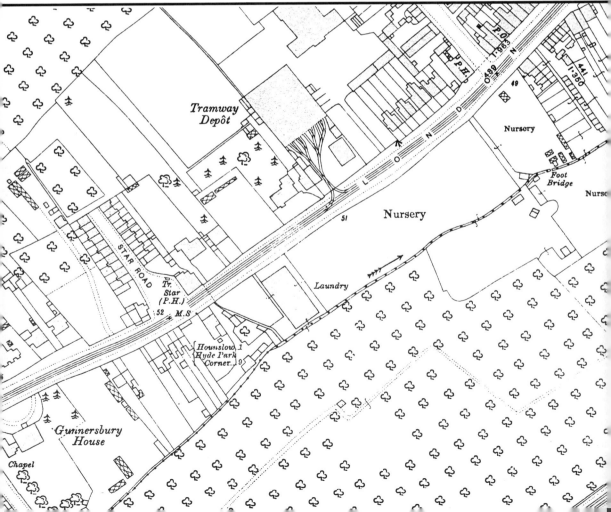

77. Construction work is still proceeding on the sub-station next to the entrance gates. Outside in London Road cars 19 and 7 are posed for the photographer.

78. On High Street, Hounslow, a carter obviously has great confidence in his horse as he stands up in the wake of a passing tramcar. Street lighting was often attached to tramway standards, but here the arc light has its own ornate support.

79. Car 86 is pictured in Hounslow Broadway on a sunny day in 1903. Note that this section of track is paved with wooden blocks. These had the effect of deadening traffic noise, and this particular method of road construction was especially favoured outside churches and other places of worship.

80. In the first decade of the twentieth century there were no parking problems in Hounslow High Street. Car 61 has an unobstructed run.

81. The Town Hall has the benefit of extra street lighting so that visiting dignitaries will be able to see where they step. This was more of a problem in those days when the natural product so beloved of rose growers was liberally distributed by the passing horse drawn traffic!

82. This card was posted on 24th August 1907. Note the green painted traction standards with cream collars, and the imposing arc lamps of the Heston and Isleworth UDC.

83. We look west towards Bell Corner, with Staines Road on the left and Bath Road on the right. This latter thoroughfare was to be used for an extension of the tramways to Cranford, Slough and Maidenhead. However the LUT's application in May 1902 for a Light Railway Order was rejected by the Light Railway Commissioners. The main objector was the powerful Great Western Railway.

84. Car 82 halts at Bell Corner, and a Bourne & Hollingsworth van takes advantage of the lull in the traffic to pull out of Bath Road. The estate agents and the posters on the right give the impression that Hounslow was a fast developing suburb.

85. The section of track from Bell Corner to Hounslow Heath was abandoned on 5th July 1922. Car 332 is positioned on the terminal stub outside the electricity showrooms. This scene dates from about 1931.

⟶

86. We pull back slightly from the terminus to observe car 261 about to return to Shepherds Bush on route 57. This vehicle was reconditioned in 1928; it received a new top deck and was reclassified type WT. From the look of it, it would seem that car 261 has just been returned from the works.

⟶

87. This view of Staines Road perhaps gives us some indication as to why traffic receipts on this stretch were rather meagre. There seems to be a marked lack of customer potential in this sparsely populated area. Car 82 maintains the service, and as it is a fine day, it may be carrying ramblers who have used Hounslow Heath as a jumping off point for their country jaunt.

88. We observe Wellington Road at the junction with Staines Road, with car 50 setting down a passenger on this last section before the terminus. This location was used from 1935 as a turning circle for the 657 trolleybuses.

89. Car 311 slows for the terminus outside The Hussar by the junction of Barrack Road, Hounslow Heath. As we can tell by the presence of car 1 in the distance, a mixed open top and covered top tram service was being offered. In inclement weather travellers would let the open toppers go past.

90. It was a proud moment for the motorman and conductor of car 11 as they posed at Hounslow Heath terminus. On the back of the photo the motorman is named as Mr. W. Bastable. This is a classic view from the tramway era when smart crews, cheap fares, frequent services (which ran on time) and clean vehicles were all the rage - what a contrast to the state of affairs nowadays!

91. This was probably a day to slake one's thirst in The Hussar before taking car 10 back to town. Note the local authority cart which was probably dampening the dust on the rudementary road surface.

92. Our penultimate view of the terminus depicts car 18 with The Light Horse Public House in the background. This tram belonged originally to type Z, and on receiving a top deck canopy in 1910-11 it was reclassified type Y. Unfortunately the canopy was constructed "on the cheap" and although the ends were glazed, passengers amidships had to put up with ill fitting roller blinds. Needless to say, the whole contraption was rather draughty, all of which earned these trams the nickname of "influenza cars"! To add insult to injury, the original floor mounted trolley standard was retained so that the trolley pole literally stuck out the roof, thereby causing an unwelcome ingress of rainwater, which became a torrent during winter gales.

93. We finish our journey in company with car 55. The LUT had great plans to continue the rails onwards to Baber Bridge and Staines, but economic realities and the hostility of the local authorities caused Sir James Clifton Robinson's noble vision to fade.

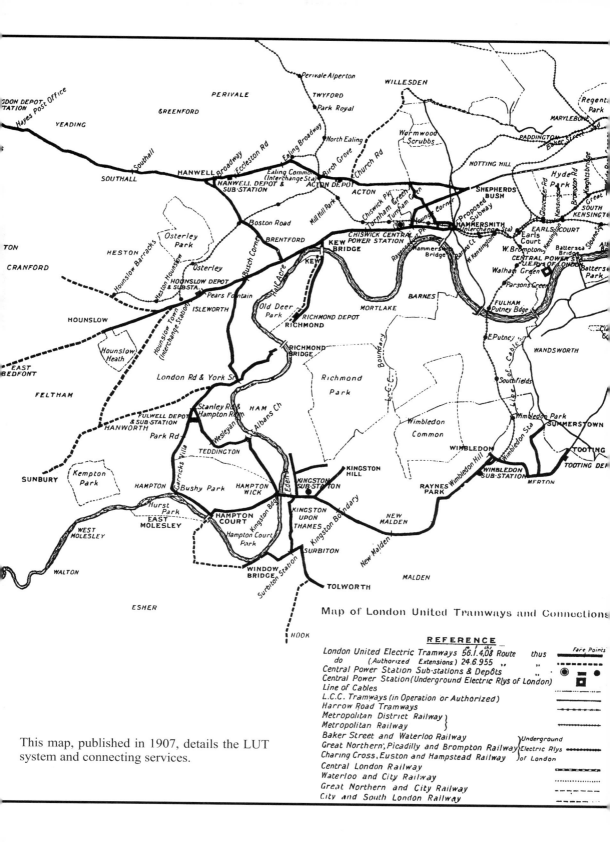

This map, published in 1907, details the LUT system and connecting services.

Map of London United Tramways and Connections

REFERENCE

			Fare Points
London United Electric Tramways 56.1.4.08 Route *thus* · · ·
do (Authorized Extensions) 24.6.955 ,,
Central Power Station Sub-stations & Depôts ,,
Central Power Station (Underground Electric Rlys of London)
Line of Cables
L.C.C. Tramways (in Operation or Authorized)
Harrow Road Tramways
Metropolitan District Railway
Metropolitan Railway } Underground
Baker Street and Waterloo Railway
Great Northern, Picadilly and Brompton Railway } Electric Rlys
Charing Cross, Euston and Hampstead Railway } of London
Central London Railway
Waterloo and City Railway
Great Northern and City Railway
City and South London Railway

LUT WORKS CARS MISCELLANY

The LUT had a small fleet of ancillary vehicles which serviced the fleet and the permanent way department.

001 Sand Van - single truck
002 Water Tank/Rail Grinder - single truck
003 Water Tank/Rail Grinder - single truck
004 Ticket Van - single truck
005 Stores Van - double truck
006 Rail Grinder (ex-SMET car 13) - single truck

94. LUT water car 002 is seen next to MET breakdown van 07 at Finchley Depot. Such interfleet loans and transfers were common amongst the "Underground Group" which included the London United, South Metropolitan and Metropolitan Electric systems.

95. Car 003 survived into LT days and it was scrapped in 1935.

96. A broadside view of car 003 shows the vehicle in London Transport ownership.

97. The winch and hoist on car 005 came in very handy when transferring heavy wheelsets between depots. The Brill 22E trucks and the lower deck chassis were salvaged from a type W car.

98. Car 005 was subsequently repainted in LT red and received Gill Sans gold fleet numerals. It was a very strange looking vehicle to encounter along the high street.

⟶

99. Outside Hanwell Depot we catch our last glimpse of car 005. Former LUT car 148 brings up the rear. The active passenger carrying life of this vehicle ended around 1910 when some of the 101-150 type X were relegated to staff car and works duties, the majority of the type, however, were stored and later scrapped.

100. Car 142 was referred to by the staff as "Noah's Ark" in recognition of its role as "flood car" for use when trams could not ford any inundated sections of track. Car 142's traction motors were raised through the floor of the lower saloon, and this car normally towed car 141 which had had its motors removed. Passengers were then accommodated in car 141. The pair worked a shuttle to the nearest dry land, where passengers were transferred to normal service cars. This service is depicted in *Twickenham and Kingston Tramways.*

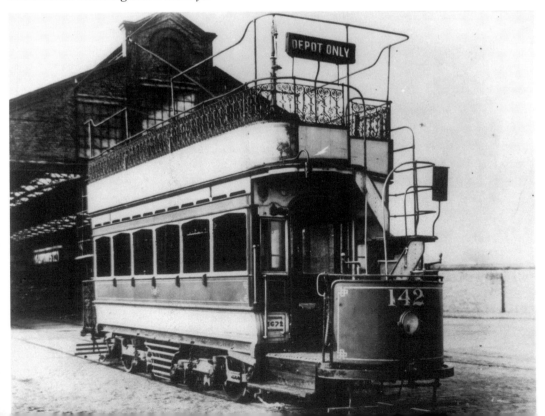

UPSTAIRS - DOWNSTAIRS

First and foremost, trams were employed to transport people from point A to point B, and it is safe to assume that 99.9% of passengers were only looking to reach their destinations safely - they were not tramway enthusiasts with an interest in the design and working of the vehicles. It is also safe to say that tramway managements were often behind the times; uncomfortable seats and open

101. First order your tramcar, then have it transported by rail to the nearest LCC tram depot - such was the fate of these lower decks which were shipped from Hurst, Nelson's factory in Motherwell to sidings at New Cross LBSCR Station. Each body was then loaded on to a horse drawn float to be carted to New Cross Depot where final assembly took place.

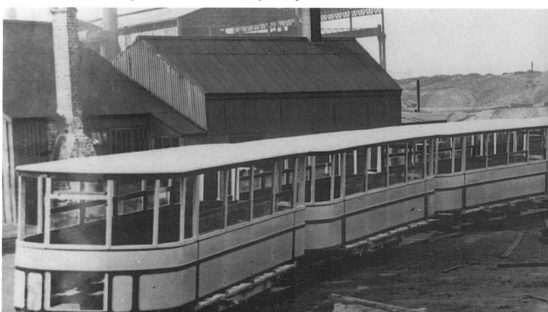

top decks were maintained for far too long. The travelling public voted with their feet and pneumatic tyre equipped buses and trolleybuses with cushioned seats began to show up the outdated qualities of many tramcars. The following section illustrates some of the changes in interior design which occurred in the metropolitan area.

102. The top decks of the class E cars were given the same treatment, which gives rise to this rather odd looking "train" outside the manufacturer's premises.

103. We view the exterior of the Prince's car complete with royal insignia on the waist panels and canopy decency boards. Swathes of ornamental green foliage were affixed over the tram's white livery.

104. On Friday, 15th May 1903, the Prince and Princess of Wales (later King George V and Queen Mary) took part in the ceremonial opening of the London County Council Tramways. This well furnished scene greeted the royal party as they travelled in the lower saloon of converted A class car 86. The LCC was certainly out to make a sumptous impression, and the effect was further enhanced by the pelmets, blue and white curtains and ruffled tie-backs. The armchairs were upholstered in pale blue which matched the carpet laid over the wooden floor.

105. What a contrast! This 1904 photo shows the everyday lower deck of a class D car. Note the long wooden benches with the patterned seat backs. Written on the bulkhead are the words PLEASE DO NOT SPIT IN THE CAR....truly a world away from pale blue cushions and thick pile carpets!

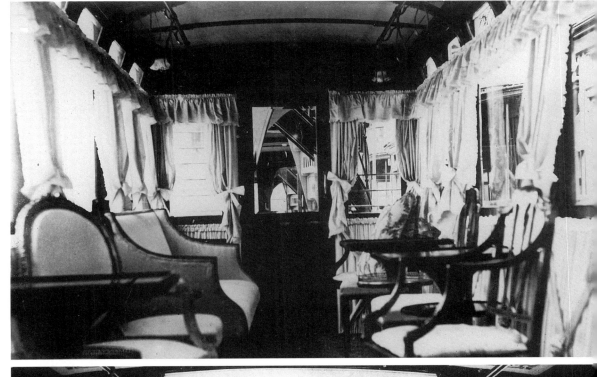

106. In the 1920s the LCC woke up to the fact that their customers needed somewhat better fixtures and fittings than the spartan finish served up by early electric tram builders. The so called "Pullmanisation" programme introduced transverse, upholstered seating to the lower saloon. Ceilings were painted white and lighting was improved so that the gentleman on the right could read his paper with ease.

107. The company run systems weren't far behind the LCC. Here we see the lower saloon of LUT car 307 which was renovated in 1925. Note the straps which lent a handhold to standing passengers at rush hours.

108. Sunlight penetrates the fastness of MET car 220, now masquerading as LT car 2265. This type G tram had seats upholstered in grey-green Moquettino. Note the bell rope which runs the length of the lower saloon ceiling.

109. Car 1989 was fitted with high back "bucket" seats in 1932. Although these added to passenger comfort, they were not liked by conductors who found it took twice as long to turn them at termini. They were also used on HR/2 cars 120, 147 and E/3 car 168.

110. "More room on top" was a common shout from harassed conductors. These "garden" type seats on the upper deck of an early LUT car do not look very inviting. On wet days the journey up here could be positively miserable, and with no provision for "dry flaps" to keep the elements from saturating the wooden seats, many a traveller would go home with a damp posterior.

111. However, when the weather was warm and the sun was out, there could be no more exhilarating place than the top deck of a tramcar. The prospect of a day out by the Thames at Hampton Court was an added inducement to enjoy the trip. The only disadvantage would be if the breeze blew your hat away, then the unfortunate gent would hail the mortorman, and the car would stop so that he could retrieve his property. The ladies on top of car 270 would have fastened their chapeaux with a fearsome looking hatpin.

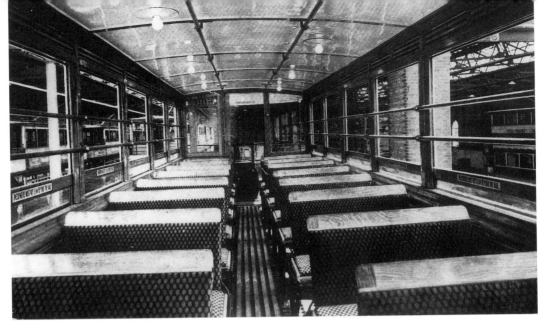

112. Enclosed upper saloons made more economic sense during bad weather. T type car 307 received upholstered seats to go with the renovated lower deck as seen in picture 107.

113. The T type were first known as "Palace" cars because in 1906 they were the most luxurious vehicles on London's streets. Time has caught up with car 320 in this late 1920s view, and it no longer represents the acme of tram building. Nevertheless, it is still a well proportioned car, built to last and offering a fair standard of passenger comfort. The only minus points are the open balconies and driver's platforms.

114. The 1931 batch of E/3 class cars delivered to the LCC for the new Kingsway Subway services had a traditional, if modernised, top deck. They retained end bulkhead doors and a somewhat cramped seating layout, although it is worth remembering that the average height of Londoners in the 1930s was less than it is now, therefore less leg room was needed.

115. The upper deck of LCC prototype car 1 gave a pleasant impression of airy spaciousness. Unfortunately London Transport came along and the tramway development programme withered on the vine. This view was taken on 3rd July 1949.

ROLLING STOCK - LUT TYPE U

Fifty cars from type W were reconditioned in 1910-11 and reclassified type U. Further improvements were effected in the succeeding years with many cars receiving magnetic brakes and higher powered motors. In 1931 ten trams of this type were loaned to the SMET where they worked the service from West Croydon to Mitcham. In December 1933 they were transferred to the Sutton route, and in 1935 all ended up at the former MET Stonebridge Park Depot. The last type U was scrapped in September 1936.

116. Car 283 is seen in 1929. Type U cars presented a solid, if rather "homemade", appearance.

117. The dashes of car 299 have been painted as a warning sign so that motorists keep their distance. This tram was later transferred to Croydon to work on the SMET lines.

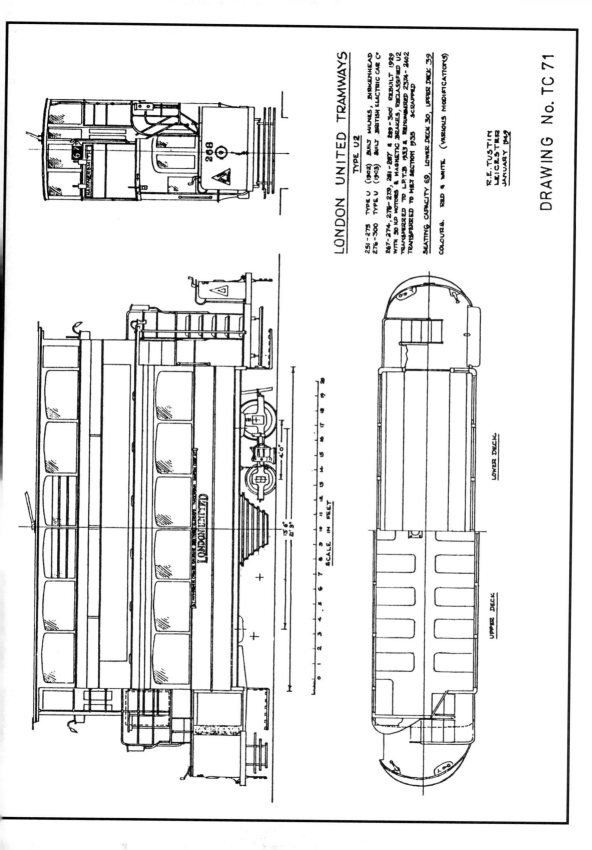

LONDON UNITED TRAMWAYS

TYPE U2

251 - 275   TYPE U (1902)   BUILT MILNES , BIRKENHEAD
276 - 300   TYPE U (1903)   BUILT BRITISH ELECTRIC CAR Cº

267 - 274, 276 - 279, 281 - 287 & 289 - 300 REBUILT 1929
WITH 50 HP MOTORS & MAGNETIC BRAKES, RECLASSIFIED U2
TRANSFERRED TO L.P.T.B. 1933 & RENUMBERED 2374 - 2402
TRANSFERRED TO METR SECTION 1935   SCRAPPED

SEATING CAPACITY 69, LOWER DECK 30, UPPER DECK 39

COLOURS. RED & WHITE. (VARIOUS MODIFICATIONS)

LONDON UNITED

268

R.E. TUSTIN
LEICESTER
JANUARY 1942

LOWER DECK

UPPER DECK

15'6"
21'9"
4'0"

SCALE IN FEET
0 1 2 3 4 5 6 7 8 9 10 11 12 13 14 15 16 17 18 19 20

DRAWING No. TC 71

118. Car 269 is caught on camera in West Croydon. There is no doubt that these LUT vehicles provided considerable assistance for the hard pressed SMET. Note that car 269 retains cream painted rocker panels.

119. Passengers alight from car 268 at the terminus in West Croydon. Ironically trams are set to return to this location, as in 1998 track was laid for the new Croydon Tramlink. The swish new, air conditioned single deckers will be the direct descendants of the trams that served Londoners so well in the past. Truly the wheel has turned full circle!

PROGRESS -
TOO LITTLE, TOO LATE!

120. With "Poppy" and the later Feltham type cars London's company owned tramways did try to stem the anti-tram tide of the 1930s. But even car 350 could not match the enthusiasm for the new trolleybuses, and the trams took their leave. In the meanwhile the streets of the metropolis have clogged up with traffic, and we await a new generation of non-polluting tramways to help clear up the mess. Sir James Clifton Robinson and the other LUT visionaries might have said - "We told you so!"

MP Middleton Press

Easebourne Lane, Midhurst, W Sussex. GU29 9AZ Tel: 01730 813169 Fax: 01730 812601
*If books are not available from your local transport stockist, order direct with cheque,
Visa or Mastercard, post free UK.*

BRANCH LINES
Branch Line to Allhallows
Branch Lines around Ascot
Branch Line to Ashburton
Branch Lines around Bodmin
Branch Line to Bude
Branch Lines around Canterbury
Branch Lines around Chard & Yeovil
Branch Line to Cheddar
Branch Lines around Cromer
Branch Lines to Effingham Junction
Branch Lines around Exmouth
Branch Line to Fairford
Branch Line to Hawkhurst
Branch Line to Hayling
Branch Lines to Horsham
Branch Line to Ilfracombe
Branch Line to Kingswear
Branch Lines to Launceston & Princetown
Branch Lines to Longmoor
Branch Line to Looe
Branch Line to Lyme Regis
Branch Lines around March
Branch Lines around Midhurst
Branch Line to Minehead
Branch Line to Moretonhampstead
Branch Lines to Newport (IOW)
Branch Line to Padstow
Branch Lines around Plymouth
Branch Line to Selsey
Branch Lines around Sheerness
Branch Line to Swanage *updated*
Branch Line to Tenterden
Branch Lines to Torrington
Branch Lines to Tunbridge Wells
Branch Line to Upwell
Branch Lines around Weymouth
Branch Lines around Wimborne
Branch Lines around Wisbech

NARROW GAUGE BRANCH LINES
Branch Line to Lynton
Branch Lines around Portmadoc 1923-46
Branch Lines around Porthmadog 1954-94
Two-Foot Gauge Survivors
Romneyrail

SOUTH COAST RAILWAYS
Ashford to Dover
Bournemouth to Weymouth
Brighton to Eastbourne
Chichester to Portsmouth
Dover to Ramsgate
Eastbourne to Hastings
Hastings to Ashford
Portsmouth to Southampton
Southampton to Bournemouth
Worthing to Chichester

SOUTHERN MAIN LINES
Bromley South to Rochester
Charing Cross to Orpington
Crawley to Littlehampton
Dartford to Sittingbourne
East Croydon to Three Bridges
Epsom to Horsham
Exeter to Barnstaple
Exeter to Tavistock
Faversham to Dover

London Bridge to East Croydon
Orpington to Tonbridge
Tonbridge to Hastings
Salisbury to Yeovil
Swanley to Ashford
Tavistock to Plymouth
Victoria to East Croydon
Waterloo to Windsor
Waterloo to Woking
Woking to Portsmouth
Woking to Southampton
Yeovil to Exeter

EASTERN MAIN LINES
Fenchurch Street to Barking

COUNTRY RAILWAY ROUTES
Andover to Southampton
Bath to Evercreech Junction
Bournemouth to Evercreech Jn.
Burnham to Evercreech Junction
Croydon to East Grinstead
Didcot to Winchester
East Kent Light Railway
Fareham to Salisbury
Frome to Bristol
Guildford to Redhill
Porthmadog to Blaenau
Reading to Basingstoke
Reading to Guildford
Redhill to Ashford
Salisbury to Westbury
Stratford Upon Avon to Cheltenham
Strood to Paddock Wood
Taunton to Barnstaple
Wenford Bridge to Fowey
Westbury to Bath
Woking to Alton
Yeovil to Dorchester

GREAT RAILWAY ERAS
Ashford from Steam to Eurostar
Clapham Junction 50 years of change
Festiniog in the Fifties
Festiniog in the Sixties
Isle of Wight Lines 50 years of change
Railways to Victory 1944-46
SECR Centenary album

LONDON SUBURBAN RAILWAYS
Caterham and Tattenham Corner
Charing Cross to Dartford
Clapham Jn. to Beckenham Jn.
East London Line
Finsbury Park to Alexandra Palace
Holborn Viaduct to Lewisham
Kingston and Hounslow Loops
Lewisham to Dartford
Lines around Wimbledon
London Bridge to Addiscombe
North London Line
South London Line
West Croydon to Epsom
West London Line
Willesden Junction to Richmond
Wimbledon to Epsom

STEAMING THROUGH
Steaming through Cornwall
Steaming through Kent

Steaming through West Hants
Steaming through West Sussex

TRAMWAY CLASSICS
Aldgate & Stepney Tramways
Barnet & Finchley Tramways
Bath Tramways
Bournemouth & Poole Tramways
Brighton's Tramways
Camberwell & W.Norwood Tramways
Clapham & Streatham Tramways
Dover's Tramways
East Ham & West Ham Tramways
Edgware and Willesden Tramways
Eltham & Woolwich Tramways
Embankment & Waterloo Tramways
Enfield & Wood Green Tramways
Exeter & Taunton Tramways
Gosport & Horndean Tramways
Greenwich & Dartford Tramways
Hammersmith & Hounslow Tramways
Hampstead & Highgate Tramways
Hastings Tramways
Holborn & Finsbury Tramways
Ilford & Barking Tramways
Kingston & Wimbledon Tramways
Lewisham & Catford Tramways
Liverpool Tramways 1. Eastern Routes
Liverpool Tramways 2. Southern Routes
Maidstone & Chatham Tramways
North Kent Tramways
Portsmouth's Tramways
Reading Tramways
Seaton & Eastbourne Tramways
Shepherds Bush & Uxbridge Tramways
Southampton Tramways
Southend-on-sea Tramways
Southwark & Deptford Tramways
Stamford Hill Tramways
Thanet's Tramways
Victoria & Lambeth Tramways
Waltham Cross & Edmonton Tramways
Walthamstow & Leyton Tramways
Wandsworth & Battersea Tramways

TROLLEYBUS CLASSICS
Croydon Trolleybuses
Bournemouth Trolleybuses
Hastings Trolleybuses
Maidstone Trolleybuses
Reading Trolleybuses
Woolwich & Dartford Trolleybuses

WATERWAY ALBUMS
Kent and East Sussex Waterways
London to Portsmouth Waterway
Surrey Waterways
West Sussex Waterways

MILITARY BOOKS and VIDEO
Battle over Portsmouth
Battle over Sussex 1940
Blitz over Sussex 1941-42
Bombers over Sussex 1943-45
Bognor at War
Military Defence of West Sussex
Secret Sussex Resistance
Sussex Home Guard
War on the Line
War on the Line VIDEO

OTHER BOOKS
Betwixt Petersfield & Midhurst
Changing Midhurst
East Grinstead Then & Now
Garraway Father & Son
Index to all Stations
South Eastern & Chatham Railways
London Chatham & Dover Railway